Our Lady, Untier of Knots
Story of a Marian Devotion

by
Miguel Cuartero Samperi

*All booklets are published thanks to the
generous support of the members of the
Catholic Truth Society*

Contents

Foreword

Praying to the Mother of the Lord is an essential part of the Catholic faith.

It is one of the first ways we learn to pray as children.

The thousands of paintings and sculptures which depict the relationship between the child Jesus and his Mother inspire feelings of tender affection in the person who turns in trust to Mary, Mother of the Christian and Mother of the Church.

There is something surprisingly simple in the way a believer reacts like a child turning spontaneously and naturally to Mary, asking for her protective gaze and maternal attention.

This is a sentiment that Christians expressed very early on through the ancient invocation: "Under your protection may we find refuge, holy Mother of God."

Marian devotion has as many faces as there are images of Mary that the faithful venerate, whether in great shrines in parish churches, in small chapels, or even in alcoves at the corners of buildings in cities and towns.

Such places are a true crossroads for Christian religious devotion, attracting both the individual believer or groups of the faithful who pause in front of them for a moment of silence, of prayer, of invocation, of help.

The everyday life of believers, their joys, sufferings and tears of sadness searching for consolation, find peace, help and hope in front of images of Mary, usually shown holding her Son in her arms.

The devotion to Mary as untier of knots, the subject of this book by Miguel Cuartero Samperi, is distinctive for a number of reasons.

First of all because the prayer emerged in Germany in the 17th century, but spread above all to Latin America through the work of then-Father Jorge Mario Bergoglio, now Pope Francis. He discovered the devotion during the time he spent studying theology in Augsburg, Germany. It is well known that as Archbishop of Buenos Aires it was his custom to attach an image of Our Lady untier of knots to his letters.

Then, there is the particularity of the prayer, which originally referred to the knots of conjugal life, the incomprehension and incompatibility that block marital life, creating ill will and bitterness. Such barriers may seriously wear down the relationship between spouses causing them to desire to separate, and thus threatening the complete breakdown of the marriage.

This prayer is addressed to Mary, that she may help spouses to overcome divisions caused by the evil one and so that the couple may once more find marital peace.

Also distinctive is the spiritual aspect of the devotion, vigorously highlighted by the then-Cardinal Bergoglio, who advised his flock to turn to Mary in order to gain a crystalline clarity in their faith in Jesus, free from such obstacles as frailty, fear, misery, selfishness that prevent us loving Jesus with a free, serene, and trusting spirit.

✠ Paolo Selvadagi
Auxiliary Bishop of Rome

History

A family in difficulty

The devotion to "Mary Untier of Knots" emerged in Germany at the beginning of the 17th century. Historical data is scarce, and not very detailed. Essentially it is a story not of a Marian apparition, but of the everyday life of a family that bears witness to the great effectiveness of prayer addressed to Mary, mediatrix of grace for mankind.

Wolfgang Langenmantel and Sophie Imhoff married in 1612, but after about three years, their marriage was in crisis, so much so that the two spouses began to consider seriously the idea of divorcing. A lack of mutual understanding and frequent arguements meant that the marriage was on the verge of breaking down altogether. Before a complete separation, however, the noble Wolfgang decided to go by foot to the nearby monastery of Ingolstadt (forty miles from Augsburg), the home of Fr Jakob Rem, a priest well known and esteemed for his discernment. Jakob Rem was the founder in Ingolstadt of a Marian congregation (*Colloquium Marianum*) that promoted devotion to Our Lady "thrice admirable". He died in 1618 and his process of beatification is underway. When Wolfgang requested his help, the Jesuit decided to entrust this grave situation to the intercession of the Blessed Mother, and together he and

Wolfgang prayed with intensity and devotion, invoking the help of Mary "thrice admirable." A painting of the Virgin of the Snows (today the patron of the city of Buenos Aires) was hanging in the monastery chapel and in front of this image Fr Jakob knelt to ask for the grace of reconciliation between the two spouses. Over the span of twenty-eight days, Wolfgang went on pilgrimage on four consecutive Saturdays to the monastery of Ingolstadt in order to lay his marriage with Sophie at the feet of the Virgin Mary. The twenty-eight days of prayer reflected the time in which a woman's body prepares to welcome a new life. It is a process that leads from death to new life. And, during this period of twenty-eight days the marriage of Wolfgang and Sophie was renewed, obtaining a new strength and vitality.

The reconciliation

Within a short time, the couple experienced the positive effects of their prayers to God, made through the mediation of Mary. Thanks to the time Wolfgang had spent with Fr Jakob in front of the altar of the Virgin Mary, the situation of the spouses gradually changed to the point of mutual reconciliation. Having avoided divorce, the spouses lived together in communion and happiness to the end of their days. The Virgin Mary had heard their plea for help, and God had granted them the grace requested.

An extraordinary event

Related to this is an extraordinary event witnessed by Fr Jakob on 28th September 1615 in the monastery chapel. Testimonies about this episode are few and confused. However, it appears that Sophie had given Fr Jakob the special ribbon used during her wedding to Wolfgang. Following local custom, the hands of both spouses had been bound together with a ribbon during their Nuptial Mass, as a sign and symbol of the indissoluble bond created between them thanks to the grace of the sacrament. After every argument with her husband, Sophie had tied a little knot in the wedding ribbon; that same ribbon, full of knots, was given to the Jesuit father for special prayers. While Fr Jakob knelt in front of the painting, he took the ribbon and prayed intensely to the Virgin Mary to untie each and every knot preventing peace between the spouses: "With this act of devotion," he said solemnly to the Virgin of the Snows, "I raise to you the ribbon of marriage; untie all of the knots and make it smooth." As Fr Jakob prayed, the knots of the ribbon miraculously fell loose, leaving it as white and brilliant as it had been on Wolfgang and Sophie's wedding day.

The moral miracle

Here the miracle is tinged with legend. Versions of the story differ in detail, as might be expected with a 300-year old story rediscovered only within the past few decades. But the true miracle, on which we should focus, is the "moral miracle" - of reconciliation and forgiveness, between two spouses on the verge of separating. Wherever forgiveness seems impossible for human beings - hindered by hatred, rancour, resentment, and pride - only God's loving intervention through Our Lady's invaluable intercession can make reconciliation possible. Often selfishness means man lives for himself alone, and this renders him incapable of opening up to another, in order to give himself completely to them. Hence the need for "moral miracles". Christ, "our Peace," makes forgiveness and full communion possible, by breaking down the wall of separation that is raised between people. Christ's victory over death is visibly made manifest, in the victory of love over hatred, of forgiveness over division (cf. *Ep* 2:14). This moral miracle of conversion of heart shone forth, as a wonderful witness, in the first Christian communities, where, through the grace of the Holy Spirit Christians were united beyond differences of social and economic class, gender, and character. Seeing this new kind of love, the pagans, amazed, exclaimed: "See how they love one another...and how they are ready to die for each other" (cf. Tertullian, *Apologeticum* 39, 7).

Through the intercession of the Virgin Mary, Wolfgang and Sophie were able to put such love into practice and forgive each other: their marriage, therefore, was saved and the Divider, defeated!

A grateful grandson

The years went by and Wolfgang and Sophie's grandson Hieronymus Ambrosius von Langenmantel (1666-1709), entered religious life and became canon of the church of Sankt Peter am Perlach in Augsburg. Hieronymus dedicated one of the church's chapels to the memory of his family, and commissioned an altarpiece as an ex voto, to commemorate the saving of his grandparents' marriage through Our Lady's intercession. The work has been attributed to the Bavarian painter Johann Melchior Georg Schmidtner, who completed the painting between 1699 and 1700. He decided to represent the Blessed Virgin of Good Counsel, but also wanted to add details that would recall the history of the Langenmantel family.

The painting depicts the Blessed Mother in heaven, among the angels. She is intent upon untying the knots in a ribbon that is held for her by an angel on her left. After untying the knots, Mary passes the untied ribbon to another angel on her right. The episode evidently recalls the miracle that took place on 28th September 1615, when the knots of the wedding ribbon were untied through the intercession of Mary. This emphasised the importance of the figure of Mary as mediatrix within the life of the couple. The Virgin is represented according to the image described in Revelation:

> "And a great portent appeared in heaven, a woman clothed with the sun, with the moon under her feet,

and on her head a crown of twelve stars; she was with child and she cried out in her pangs of birth, in anguish for delivery." (*Rv* 12:1-2)

Mary, the new Eve, crushes the head of the serpent with her foot, fulfilling and making present the prophecy made to the serpent in Genesis: "She shall bruise your head, and you shall bruise his heel" (*Gn* 3:15). There is a beautiful detail at the bottom of the picture: the archangel Raphael appears accompanying Tobias to the meeting with his wife. The story is taken from the Old Testament, from the book of Tobit (cf. *Tb* 5-7), which narrates the adventure of Tobias and Sarah, who were united in marriage through the divine intervention manifested in the presence of the angel. The image of Tobias and the angel is intended to emphasise even more that marriage is desired and brought to a good end by God, who sends his angels to help the couple on their journey. One can also read this scene as containing a veiled allusion to Wolfgang Langenmantel, who, accompanied by his guardian angel, is walking toward the Jesuit monastery to ask for help from God in his time of crisis. According to the tradition, along the way Wolfgang encountered a fisherman called *Engel* ("angel" in German) who was walking with his dog. The fisherman gave Wolfgang directions to the monastery and then vanished without a trace. Because of his role and his mysterious identity, this fisherman is identified by pious legend as an angel sent by God.

The image of Mary intent on untying the knots cannot help but recall the expression of St Irenaeus, Bishop of Lyons (who died in the year 202). In his treatise *Against the Heresies*, St Irenaeus affirmed: "The knot of Eve's disobedience found a solution through the obedience of Mary. That which Eve had bound by her incredulity, Mary untied by her faith" (Adv. Haer. 3, 22, 4; cf. CCC 494). We can speculate that the author of the painting was inspired by the words of the holy father of the Church, even if there is no evidence of a direct connection with the patristic text.

One final detail concerns the mantle of the Virgin Mary, a blue cloak blowing in the wind. In Sacred Scripture, the Holy Spirit is often represented as a breeze, a divine breath or strong wind (cf. *Ac* 2:2). The Virgin Mary, present at the moment of Pentecost and filled with the Holy Spirit (cf. CCC 724), is represented enveloped by the wind of the Spirit, which is also symbolised by the dove flying above her head. One unofficial interpretation suggests the painter took the idea of the long mantle from the last name of the patrons, the Langenmantels, which in German means "long mantle."

A devotion is born

After the Langenmantels' marital problems had been overcome, and an altar set up to the Virgin Mary in the Church of St Peter, a unique devotion to Our Lady began to grow there.

The faithful began to turn to her, especially with family problems. However, for roughly two centuries the image, though enjoying modest popularity in Germany, remained almost unknown in the rest of the world. In Germany, this devotion was known as *Maria Knotenlöserin*.

Spread of the devotion: Cardinal Bergoglio

Only in the 20th century did this Marian devotion emerge from Germany to become known in the rest of the world. The current Pope Francis was responsible for bringing the image to Latin America where it was rebaptised *la desatanudos* or *la desatadora de nudos*.

Fr Jorge Mario Bergoglio fell in love with this devotion as soon as he discovered it, in the 1980s. In 1986, he had gone to Augsburg to complete his thesis on the German theologian Romano Guardini. During his stay in Germany, far from his country and family, Bergoglio visited the church of Sankt Peter am Perlach, overseen by his Jesuit confrères. It was there that he saw for the first time that unique painting of the Virgin Mary, heard about its story and the devotion, and decided to take the image to Buenos Aires as a gift for his parishioners. Just like a parent bringing back a gift for his or her children on their return from a trip abroad, Bergoglio decided to bring back to Argentina some copies of that beautiful image of Mary, with the aim of spreading the devotion in Argentina. Once home, Bergoglio began to distribute the images to the priests and faithful, and Mary untier of knots was welcomed with great enthusiasm by the faithful of South America. From Buenos Aires the devotion rapidly spread first to other Argentine cities and then to other countries of Latin America.

The Blessed Mother untier of knots in Argentina

One of the images brought by Jorge Mario Bergoglio to Buenos Aires was placed in the rectory of the Colegio del Salvador, the Jesuit school founded in the Argentine capital in 1868. In 1996, with the permission of the Archbishop of Buenos Aires at the time, Cardinal Antonio Quarracino, Fr Rodolfo Arroyo, the parish priest of San José del Talar, decided to spread the devotion to Mary untier of knots in the parish, which is located in the Agronomía quarter, northwest of the Argentine capital, and which stands on what were the first Jesuit estates before the Society was expelled from South America in 1767. Fr Arroyo dedicated an altar to the Virgin "untier of knots" and her image was placed in a chapel on the lefthand side of the church; the painting, a work of the Argentine painter Ana María Betta de Berti (who received the image of the Virgin from the hands of Bergoglio), was enthroned on 8th December, 1996, the solemnity of the Immaculate Conception. In 2010, Cardinal Bergoglio, the Archbishop of Buenos Aires, elevated the parish of San José to the dignity of a shrine: today, in Buenos Aires, the parish of San José (previously known for devotion to St Vitus, a 3rd century Sicilian martyr) is also known as the *Santuario de Nuestra Señora la que desata los nudos*. Increasing numbers of the faithful come every month to greet this beautiful image, asking Mary to protect their families. On the eighth day of every month, hundreds of pilgrims gather to celebrate the feast of Mary untier of knots. On December 8th of every year, on the solemn feast of the Immaculate Conception, hundreds of devotees from different parts of the country gather in the streets of Agronomía to venerate the image of Our Lady untier of knots. On these occasions the priests of San José have to celebrate Mass outside in order to permit the many faithful to participate more fully in the Eucharistic liturgy.

The Cardinal's words

On 8th December 2011, Cardinal Bergoglio celebrated Holy Mass at San José del Talar on the occasion of the fifteenth anniversary of the enthronement of the image at the shrine. In the homily, he affirmed:

> "We all have knots, or deficiencies in our hearts, and we go through difficulties. God, our good Father, who distributes his grace to all of his children, wants us to trust Her, to entrust to Her the knots of our sins, the tangles of our miseries that prevent us from uniting ourselves with God, to allow Her to untie them and bring us to Her son Jesus."

Mary and Pope Francis

Since Bergoglio has become Pope Francis, this devotion that the Holy Father himself helped to promote, has gained immediate worldwide diffusion. Now the novena has been translated into eight languages and is available on every continent. Pope Francis has demonstrated his profound devotion to the Virgin Mary right from the moment he was elected pontiff, so much so that on the first day of his pontificate he wanted to visit the Roman basilica of St Mary Major (home of the well-known image of Mary Salus Populi Romani), to entrust his new mission to God. This is how he began his Petrine ministry, putting everything, including the tightest knots, those which only she can untie and free into the capable hands of Mary. The basilica of St Mary Major, the first church dedicated to the Mother of God in the Christian West, was founded in the 5th century on the Esquiline hill in the place of the miraculous snowfall of 5th August 358 (the origin of the name of Santa Maria ad Nives). St Mary of the Snows is also the patron of Buenos Aires, and it was precisely in front of a copy of the image of the Virgin of the Snows that, four hundred years before, Wolfgang Langenmantel had prayed with devotion in the monastery of Ingolstadt to save his marriage with Sophie. Wolfgang's spiritual director, the Jesuit Father Jakob Rem, during his stay in the city of Rome became profoundly devoted to the Blessed Mother of the Snows of St Mary Major.

The novena that defeats the devil

The novena to Mary untier of knots is also known as the novena "that defeats the devil." In fact, according to the Capuchin exorcist Fr Cipriano de Meo, it was the devil himself, during an exorcism, who confessed that it was that novena - recited by the wife of a possessed man - which destroyed the murderous plan concerning her unfortunate husband. From that moment the exorcist advised all of his "patients" to pray to Mary precisely through this unique devotion that destroys the plans of the devil. In the book *La Vergine Maria e il diavolo negli esorcismi* (Paoline, 2010), the exorcist Francesco Bamonte, emphasising Mary's fundamental role in the fight against the devil, affirmed:

"Then there are Marian devotions that are particularly unbearable to the demons...Among these is the Ave Maria, the daily offering of Saint Bonaventure, and the Rosary" (p. 31).

Fr Gabriele Amorth has also emphasised Mary's role saying:

"One touches with one's hands how Mary is Mediatrix of grace, because it is always she who obtains liberation from her Son liberation from the demon."

In the book of Genesis, God condemns the serpent to being defeated by the offspring of the woman (cf. *Gn* 3:15). Between the serpent and the woman there is enmity, a battle represented poetically in the last book of the Bible (cf. *Rv* 12). But in this battle the woman is the victor through the power granted to her by God. This is why the Immaculate Conception, as also Our Lady untier of knots, is represented by Mary crushing with her foot the head of the serpent, a symbol of the evil that threatens the life of every man.

The testimony of an exorcist

With regard to the relationship between the novena to Mary untier of knots and the devil, Capuchin Father Cipriano de Meo, an exorcist, relates the following:

"One Friday I was at an exorcism Mass in Torre Le Nocelle (Avellino). In front of me a possessed woman was reacting to the prayers with loud screaming and yelling. The demon, through her, was complaining about a scorching defeat, repeating like a broken record: 'I was supposed to blow that man's brains out, but She saved him!' And then, referring to the Blessed Mother, whose name he never pronounced, he added with rage: 'It was that Woman who ruined me! It was that novena, that accursed novena that saved him!! The novena to that Woman!!! Of all the novenas that his wife recited for him, that was the most powerful, that was the one that saved him!!!' The whining went on endlessly, prompting in me, needless to say, a substantial interest. What novena could have been so powerful as to have destroyed a plan of death? I wondered. In my mind I reviewed the most famous Marian novenas, but the demon was not providing any information to identify the one that had defeated him. I consoled myself by thinking that any prayer to the Virgin Mary has a devastating impact on the kingdom of darkness, and that therefore this statement was an encouragement to implore her more often. But I was not giving up: I wanted to know! So I began to beseech the Lord in my heart, that he might require satan to reveal through the mouth of that possessed woman the name of the novena that had shattered his plans, and in the end, to my great surprise, he heard me.

"Toward the end of the exorcism, the demon revealed: 'It is the novena to "She who unties the knots" that has destroyed my plans and has saved him! I was supposed to blow his brains out! It is the most powerful novena among all those which his wife recited, she had already done so many, but this one ruined me!' Finally, by divine permission, I knew what novena to recommend to all!" (Patrizia Cattaneo, *Il diavolo in ginocchio*, Segno, 2007)

Our Lady untier of knots and the family

The devotion to Mary untier of knots has been, since its origin, closely connected to marriage and the family, as it was to save the indissoluble bond between two spouses that the Virgin Mary desired to manifest her closeness and the efficacy of her intercession.

Mary untier of knots is therefore invoked above all for family problems: marital crises, incomprehension, infidelity, separations and divisions between spouses, problems of every kind with the children, disputes between siblings, risky pregnancies, violence in the family, illnesses, work problems and other kinds of difficult situations that, like small and large knots to be untied, make family life a cluster of tangles.

The Virgin Mary, spouse of Joseph and Mother of Jesus, fully understands the problems and difficulties of a family. Let us turn to her to obtain the virtues necessary so that our families may follow the footsteps of the Holy Family of Nazareth, where Jesus found a safe and welcoming home.

In the Gospel of John (cf. *Jn* 2:1-11), Mary is the one who asks Jesus to intervene in the marriage. In Cana of Galilee, in fact, during a wedding banquet, the wine - sign of joy and gladness - runs out. Mary, noticing the problem, immediately turns to Jesus with the solicitude of a loving mother saying: "They have no more wine." The mediation of Mary is precious in every marriage; let us turn to her, Queen of the family, in the moment of need, when the wine of joy runs out, so that she may call Jesus and urge him to manifest his glory.

Christian marriage, a visible and efficacious sign of the Covenant between Christ and men, is often threatened, especially in modern-day society, by numerous internal and external dangers. This is why, in the face of the wounds and divisions provoked by sin, there is so great a need for the help of God's grace - of which Mary is Mediatrix - without which marriage, an "intimate community of life and love" (*Familiaris Consortio*, no. 50), risks succumbing (cf. CCC 1606-1608).

The Blessed Mother untier of knots in Rome

Mary untier of knots is venerated in Rome at the church of Santa Anastasia al Palatino. For several years, since 2006, the novena has been prayed at this church, which is known for being the first Roman parish to have offered perpetual Eucharistic adoration, day and night.

On 20th October 2012, an image of Mary untier of knots painted by the Roman artist Simone Valariano was solemnly enthroned in the chapel of the Most Holy Sacrament. For several years, every Saturday, from 2:30 to 3 a.m., many faithful from Rome and the surrounding area have gathered at this church to recite the Rosary, asking for the intercession of Mary untier of knots. There are increasing testimonies of believers who have received benefits, spiritual graces, and have experienced the intervention of Mary in untying their personal or family knots.

Prayers to Our Lady Untier of Knots

The Supplication

Virgin Mary, Mother of fair Love,
Mother who has never abandoned
a child who cries for help,
Mother whose hands work without ceasing
for her children so beloved,
because they are impelled by divine love
and by the infinite mercy that issues from your heart,
turn to me your gaze of compassion.
Look at the many "knots" of my life.
You know my desperation and my pain.
You know how these "knots" paralyse me, Mary,
Mother charged by God with untying the "knots"
of the lives of your children,
I place the ribbon of my life in your hands.
In your hands there is no "knot" that may not be untied.
Almighty Mother, with your grace
and power of intercession
with your Son Jesus, my Saviour,
receive today this "knot" (*name it if possible...*).
For the glory of God I ask you to untie it
and to untie it always.
I hope in you.

You are the only consoler that God has given me.
You are the strength of my precarious powers,
the richness of my miseries,
the liberation of all that prevents me
from being with Christ.
Accept my plea.
Preserve me, guide me, protect me, be my refuge.
Mary untier of knots, pray for me.

Prayer

Mary, new Eve, Mother of Christ
and Mother of the Church,
you who crush the head of the ancient serpent,
you who at the proclamation of the angel
welcomed in your womb the Saviour,
you who in Bethlehem gave birth to the Creator,
who preserved in your heart
that which you could not understand,
you who in Cana of Galilee
asked for us the wine of joy,
you who, in silence, adored Christ on the cross,
you who received the Holy Spirit in the Upper Room,
untie the knots of our human misery.
Untie the knots of our sins,
of our pride, arrogance,
greed, indulgence,
envy, and sloth.

Teach us to love your Son
as you have loved him.
Intercede for us who are sinners,
now and at the hour of our death.
Amen.

Prayer of Cardinal Bergoglio

*Prayer to Mary untier of knots spread with the imprimatur
of then-Archbishop of Buenos Aires Bergoglio*

Holy Mary,
full of the Presence of God,
during the days of your earthly life
you accepted in all humility the will of the Father,
and the Evil One was never able to ensnare you
with his confusions.
Already together with your Son you interceded
for our difficulties
and with all simplicity and patience
you gave us the example of how to disentangle
the tangle of our lives.
And remaining always as Our Mother
you arrange and reveal to us
the bonds that unite us with the Lord.
Holy Mary, Mother of God and our Mother,
you who with a maternal heart untie the knots
that constrict our lives,
we ask you to receive into your hands (*name it if possible...*)

and free us from the bonds and confusions
with which our enemy torments us.
By your grace, by your intercession,
with your example free us from all evil,
our Lady, and untie the knots
that prevent us from being united with God
so that, free from all confusion and error,
we may encounter him in all things,
rest our hearts in him,
and serve him always in our brothers.
Amen.

Prayer to Mary, by Pope Francis

Recitation of the Holy Rosary at the conclusion of the Marian month, Vatican City, 31st May 2013

Mary, woman of listening,
open our ears;
grant us to know
how to listen to the word of your Son Jesus
among the thousands of words of this world;
grant that we may listen to the reality in which we live,
to every person we encounter,
especially those who are poor, in need, in hardship.

Mary, woman of decision,
illuminate our mind and our heart,
so that we may obey, unhesitating,

the word of your Son Jesus;
give us the courage to decide,
not to let ourselves be dragged along,
letting others direct our life.

Mary, woman of action,
obtain that our hands and feet move "with haste"
    toward others,
to bring them the charity and love of your Son Jesus,
to bring the light of the Gospel to the world,
as you did.
Amen.

The Novena

Sign of the Cross

In the name of the Father,
and of the Son, and of the Holy Spirit.
Amen.

Our Father

Our Father who art in heaven,
hallowed be thy name.
Thy kingdom come.
Thy will be done
on earth as it is in heaven.
Give us this day our daily bread,
and forgive us our trespasses,
as we forgive those who trespass against us,
and lead us not into temptation,
but deliver us from evil.
Amen.

Hail Mary

Hail Mary,
full of grace,
the Lord is with thee;
blessed art thou among women,
and blessed is the fruit of thy womb, Jesus.

Holy Mary,
Mother of God,
pray for us sinners,
now and at the hour of our death.
Amen.

Gloria

Glory be to the Father, and to the Son,
    and to the Holy Spirit,
as it was in the beginning, is now, and ever shall be,
world without end.
Amen.

Act of Contrition

O my God, I am heartily sorry for having offended You
and I detest all my sins, because I dread the loss of
    heaven and the pains of hell,
but most of all because they offend You, my God,
who are all good and deserving of all my love.
I firmly resolve, with the help of Your grace,
to confess my sins, to do penance and to amend my life.
Amen.

Recite the first three decades of the Holy Rosary.

Meditation for the first day

Holy Mother my beloved, holy Mary,
who unties the "knots" that oppress your children,
reach out your merciful hands to me.
I give you today this "knot" (*name it if possible...*)
and every negative consequence
that it provokes in my life.
I give you this "knot" that torments me,
makes me unhappy and prevents me
from uniting myself with you and your Son Jesus
    the Saviour.
I turn to you, Mary, who unties knots
because I trust in you
and know that you have never disdained
a sinful child who pleads with you to help him.
I believe that you can untie these knots
because you are my Mother.
I know that you will do so because you love me
    with eternal love.
Thank you, my beloved Mother.

"Mary untier of knots," pray for me.

ভ

Those who seek grace will find it in the hands of Mary.

Recite the last two decades of the Holy Rosary.

Meditation for the second day

Mary, Mother most beloved, full of grace,
my heart turns to you today.
I acknowledge that I am a sinner and need you.
I have not kept in mind your graces
because of my egoism,
my rancour, my lack
of generosity and humility.
I turn to you today,
"Mary untier of knots,"
that you may ask for me
from your Son Jesus purity of heart,
detachment, humility, and trust.
I will live this day with these virtues.
I will offer them to you as proof of my love for you.
I place this "knot" (*name it if possible...*)
in your hands
because it is preventing me from seeing the glory of God.

"Mary untier of knots," pray for me.

ങ

Mary offered to God every instant of her life.

Recite the last two decades of the Holy Rosary.

Meditation for the third day

Mother mediatrix, Queen of heaven,
in whose hands are the riches of the King,
turn to me your eyes of mercy.
I place in your holy hands this "knot"
of my life (*name it if possible...*)
and all the rancour that results from it.
God the Father, I ask you forgiveness for my sins.
Help me now to forgive every person
who knowingly or unknowingly
has provoked this "knot."
Thanks to this decision you will be able to untie it.
My beloved Mother, before you,
and in the name of your Son Jesus
my Saviour, who has been so greatly offended,
and who has been able to forgive,
I now forgive these persons...
and also myself, forever.
"Mary untier of knots," I thank you
because you untie in my heart
the "knot" of rancour
and the "knot" that I present to you today.

"Mary untier of knots," pray for me.

ᘓ

Anyone who wants graces should turn to Mary.
Recite the last two decades of the Holy Rosary.

Meditation for the fourth day

My beloved holy Mother,
who welcome all those who seek you,
have pity on me.
I place in your hands this "knot" (*name it if possible...*).
It prevents me from being happy,
from living in peace,
my soul is paralysed
and it prevents me from walking
towards my Lord and serving him.
Untie this "knot" of my life,
O my Mother.
Ask Jesus for the healing
of my paralysed faith
that stumbles over the stones in my path.
Walk with me,
my beloved Mother,
that I may be aware
that in reality these stones are for my benefit;
may I cease to complain and learn to give thanks,
to smile at every moment,
because I trust in you.

"Mary untier of knots," pray for me.

ଔ

Mary is the sun and the whole world benefits from her warmth.
Recite the last two decades of the Holy Rosary.

Meditation for the fifth day

"Mother who unties knots," you who are generous
and full of compassion,
I turn to you to place, once again,
this "knot" into your hands (*name it if possible*...).
I ask you for the wisdom of God,
that I may succeed
in the light of the Holy Spirit
in untying this tangle of difficulties.
No one has ever seen you angry;
on the contrary, your words
are so full of sweetness that in you
we meet the Holy Spirit.
Free me from the bitterness,
from the anger and hatred
that this "knot" has caused me.
My beloved Mother, give me your sweetness
and your wisdom,
teach me to meditate in the silence of my heart
and just as you did on the day of Pentecost,
intercede with Jesus
that I may receive the Holy Spirit.

"Mary untier of knots," pray for me.

ⳬ

Mary is powerful in the presence of God.
Recite the last two decades of the Holy Rosary.

Meditation for the sixth day

Queen of mercy,
I give you this "knot" of my life (*name it if possible...*)
and I ask you to give me a heart
that may know how to be patient
until you untie this "knot."
Teach me to listen to the Word of your Son,
to confess, to receive communion;
stay with me, Mary.
Prepare my heart to celebrate with the angels
the grace that you are obtaining for me.

"Mary untier of knots," pray for me.

ଔ

You are most beautiful, Mary, and there is no stain in you.

Recite the last two decades of the Holy Rosary.

Meditation for the seventh day

Mother most pure, I turn to you today: I beseech you
to untie this "knot" of my life (*name it if possible...*)
and to free me from the influence of evil.
God has granted you great power
over all the demons.
Today I renounce the demons and all of the ties
I have had with them.

I proclaim that Jesus is my only Saviour
and my only Lord.
O "Mary untier of knots,"
crush the head of the devil.
Destroy the traps caused
by these "knots" in my life.
Thank you, Mother most beloved.
Lord, free me with your precious Blood!

"Mary untier of knots," pray for me.

ଔ

You are the glory of Jerusalem, you are the honour of our people.
Recite the last two decades of the Holy Rosary.

Meditation for the eighth day

Virgin Mother of God, rich in mercy,
have pity on me, your child,
and untie the "knots" (*name them if possible...*)
of my life.
I need you to visit me,
as you did with Elizabeth.
Bring to me Jesus, bring to me the Holy Spirit.
Teach me courage, joy,
humility, and like Elizabeth
fill me with the Holy Spirit.
I want you to be my Mother,
my Queen, and my friend.

I give you my heart and all that belongs to me:
my home, my family,
my spiritual and material possessions.
I belong to you forever.
Give me a heart like yours so that I may do
all that Jesus tells me to do.

"Mary untier of knots," pray for me.

ભ

Let us walk full of trust toward the throne of grace.

Recite the last two decades of the Holy Rosary.

Meditation for the ninth day

Mary Most Holy, our advocate,
you who untie "knots,"
I come to you today to thank you for having untied
this "knot" (*name it if possible...*)
in my life.
You know the sadness it has caused me.
Thank you, my beloved Mother, I thank you
because you have untied the "knots" of my life.
Enfold me in your mantle of love,
protect me, illuminate me with your peace.

"Mary untier of knots," pray for me.

Recite the last two decades of the Holy Rosary.